Devotions
for
Young Teens

Devotions
for Young Teens

HELEN F. COUCH
and
SAM S. BAREFIELD

ABINGDON PRESS
NASHVILLE • NEW YORK

Contents

DEVOTIONS FOR YOUNG TEENS

A Word Before I Pray

Now I stop and come to speak to God.
  Quiet, world.
  Quiet, mind.
  Quiet, all.
For first I must listen.
And then I must wait.
And then, if he speaks first,
Perhaps I'll have a word to say.

  Quiet, world.
  Quiet, mind.
  Quiet, all.
    I must listen. . . .

How Can I Be Sure?

DO YOU EVER JUST BOG DOWN IN FRUSTRATION AND discouragement? There are so many decisions to be made, so many choices that will not only affect your life today but also the future. You keep asking yourself, How can I be sure?

We can't be sure, of course. No one at any age can be absolutely sure that he will make the right choices every day. But we can all take a clue from the way Jesus handled his decisions.

At each turning point or crisis in his life Jesus prayed. The Gospel of Luke tells us that he prayed at the time of his baptism. He also prayed before he selected his disciples. He prayed as he healed the sick and ministered to those who were in need or in trouble. He prayed when he taught others how to pray, before the crucifixion and, finally, on the cross. Each time he was faced with making a choice, he turned aside from what he was doing and prayed for guidance.

We, too, can find help in making our choices if we pause long enough for a quiet time of prayer. In silence we can go over the choices that are open to us, one by one. We can think out the possible results of each choice, both good and bad. Sometimes we may even

9

take paper and pencil and list these possible results, carefully weighing one against the other as we think about them. We can ask God's guidance, ask him to help us make the choice that is right for us. And we can listen quietly for his direction.

Do you have an important choice to make today or in the very near future? If so, you will want to spend some time today in quiet thought and prayer.

Ask yourself: What choices are open to me? What will each of these choices mean to me? Now? Later? How will each of these possible choices affect my friendships? My parents? Which choices are in keeping with what I think is right for a Christian?

Be still, and know that I am God. (Ps. 46:10.)

O God, I am grateful for this opportunity to turn to you in prayer today. Help me make the right choice. And help me remember always that I need more than my own understanding if I am to choose wisely. AMEN.

you'll choose well if you . . .

Choose Life!

DO YOU REMEMBER THE ONE ABOUT A FRIEND ASKING the centipede how he knew which foot to use? Suddenly Old Thousand-legs became flustered. He became so conscious of the process of walking that he couldn't decide how to take his next step, and he stumbled all over himself until he tumbled into the ditch—where he was last seen staring at his feet!

He won't move again, you can be sure, until he can decide which foot to start on. Decisions often throw us, and they demand our full attention until we are sure we are ready to move—on the right foot. Moses pointed this out to the people he was trying to lead away from their troubles. He reminded them they had the choice of drifting along, stewing in their own confusion, or they could choose life and begin to help determine the direction their lives should take.

I call heaven and earth to witness against you this day, that I have set before you life and death, blessing and curse; therefore choose life, that you and your descendants may live, loving the Lord your God, obeying his voice, and cleaving to him; for that means life to you and length of days, that you may dwell in the land which the Lord swore to your fathers. (Deut. 30:19-20.)

Choose life! Are you ready to understand what that will mean to you—what it will give you? What it will demand from you?

Choose life! Before you lies the whole world, God's creation. Can you reach out and embrace it in his name

11

without forgetting that both you and the world belong to him?

Choose life! Do you realize that the choice is before you, just as it was before the Hebrew people as Moses led them? Do you know that choosing life, instead of turning your back upon it and shunning it, will change all your ways?

Choose life! Decide to live *your* life as a follower of Jesus, who came to bring us life in its fullest abundance.

O God, lead me as I try to understand what it means to affirm life—to open my whole being to your love. In the name of Christ I pray. AMEN.

sometimes you have to play . . .

Second Fiddle

"WHAT IS THE MOST DIFFICULT PART OF YOUR WORK?" a newspaper reporter asked a prominent orchestra director.

"Finding musicians who are willing to play second fiddle," was his prompt reply. "There are plenty of first violinists, but no one wants to play second."

This business of playing second fiddle isn't limited to

musicians, is it? Most of us would rather be the first violinist. We would rather be out in front, the most popular, the leader in whatever is going on, the one who is in the spotlight when something exciting is happening. But this isn't always possible. Sometimes—although we hate to admit it—we just don't have what it takes to be first. Someday, maybe—but not now. Perhaps never. Each of us has his particular talents, his unique personality, his own way of working with others. Sometimes we do our best under the leadership of another person—that is, we do a better job of playing second fiddle than we would if we had responsibility for playing first violin. And sometimes the end result, the goal we are striving for, is possible only when we support another person—when we do play second fiddle.

Actually, the question of whether or not we will play second fiddle isn't nearly as important as the question, How will we play it? If we are doing our best, giving full cooperation to the one playing first, and staying with it through thick and thin, then we are turning in a good performance. And—who knows? The time may come when this experience at second fiddle may mean we are ready to move up to first chair.

Spend some time today thinking about your various interests and activities—schoolwork, sports, church activities, music or drama groups, hobbies, and so forth.

13

Do you "play first violin" in any of these? Or second fiddle? If you play second fiddle, how do you play it— cheerfully? without resentment? to the best of your ability? with the purpose of helping others?

Don't cherish exaggerated ideas of yourself or your importance, but try to have a sane estimate of your capabilities by the light of the faith that God has given you all. (Rom. 12:6, Phillips.)

O God, help me remember that being a Christian in all of living often demands that I play second fiddle. Help me remember, too, that greater things for thee can be accomplished when I carry the part of any responsibility that I am best fitted for and when I do my part well. AMEN.

maybe you're not . . .

Asking the Right Questions

"THEM THAT ASKS NO QUESTIONS ISN'T TOLD A LIE."

Kipling is right, all right. But he might have said it the *other* way around:

"Them that asks no questions never get an answer."

There was a time when young people's questions

were not welcomed, since most grown-ups felt that they were either obnoxious or a sign of ignorance—and besides, children should be seen and not heard!

But today most adults encourage young people to ask questions, and most young people take them up on the offer. *Those who make the most out of growing up are those who learn to ask the right questions.*

Actually, it is a lot more important for you to ask the right questions than for you to know all the answers. If you know what you want to find out, you can get help in finding answers. But if your questions about life and its meaning are fuzzy and useless, not to mention pointless, the answers you get will not make much difference in your life.

Jesus, when he was just about your age, went with his parents to the Temple in Jerusalem. What astonished the wisest men there was not what Jesus taught them. *They were astounded that a young man of his age could ask so many important questions.* You can very well imagine him strolling around the courtyard pointing out odd objects and asking about them. But that would not have surprised anyone. When he began to ask about how we know God, about how he could learn to tell others about God's love, and about what the Bible meant—that is when the leaders got excited.

In the days of your youth, you are still asking questions and not handing out many answers. A Christian

15

—all his life—continues to seek the truth, asking always for more and more light. He learns to ask the *right* questions, the important questions. And then he finds that as he lives his life, the right people with the right answers come along and help him learn what life is all about.

Maybe it is your question-asking ability that gives you an edge over the adults around you. And maybe the reason you have some insights that grown-ups are apt to forget is due to the fact that God can answer persons who ask the right questions.

Jesus once thanked God for this very fact:

I thank thee, Father, Lord of heaven and earth, that thou hast hidden these things from the wise and understanding and revealed them to babes. (Matt. 11:25.)

Today, ask God to help you ask the right questions. And ask him also to help you all your life to remember that he can answer you only if you seek his truth.

16

when you wonder about . . .

Being a Witness

YOU'VE WATCHED COURTROOM SCENES ON TV, HAVEN'T you? You remember that both the attorney for the defense and the prosecuting attorney bring in a number of witnesses. As each of the witnesses is questioned, he gives information that is intended to help prove a certain point in the case. Little by little the testimony of the witnesses piles up the evidence for or against the defendant.

In a sense we are witnesses too. We do not have to take the stand in a crowded courtroom to give our testimony. Instead, we become witnesses to what we believe in everything we say and do. Our speech and our actions pile up the evidence—and tell people whether or not we are Christians.

For example, when we try to do our best, when we refuse to cheat in any way, when we are courteous and show respect for the rights of others, when we go out of our way to make life happier or more comfortable for another person, either close to us or at a distance, when we refuse to lower our standards of conduct to be one of the crowd—then we are really witnessing to our belief in the teachings of Jesus Christ. We are telling others that we are trying to follow his example—not just on Sunday, but on every day of the week.

Think about this business of witnessing in everyday living. What about today—have I done anything today that will tell others I am a Christian? Have I backed down when I might have witnessed for Christ? What about tomorrow? Is anything coming up where I can foresee a need for witnessing as a Christian? Do I need to think about what I will do and say?

And you shall be my witnesses in Jerusalem and in all Judea and Samaria and to the end of the earth. (Acts 1:8b.)

Forgive me, Father, when I do not have the courage to let others know where I stand as a Christian. Forgive me when I settle for being a yes-person instead of being a Christian witness. Give me the know-how to witness effectively and the courage to witness when the situation is difficult. But keep me always from being smug or feeling superior to others. AMEN.

open your eyes and see . . .

What's Going on Around You

ONE DAY A GROUP OF YOUNGSTERS FROM THE COLUMBIA Lighthouse for the Blind took a trip to "see" the District of Columbia baseball stadium. All their lives they had *heard* ball games, but on this special day they were unusually excited. One fellow named Mike said he had always wanted to step off the distance from home plate to first base, so he would have an idea how far the batter has to run. The center fielder, Jimmy Piersall, took his hand and together they stepped it off—and then stepped it off again. Another visitor, Willie, asked if he could touch a real base, and when he did, he was silent for a few moments, stroking it, feeling it, letting his hand rest on it. "I never really knew what a base was like before. It's bigger than I thought."

You may never have stopped to wonder what a base looked like, or how far it is from home to first—because you have seen a baseball diamond many times. Or at least you *think* you have. Very often those of us who have good sight take the world around us for granted, and the result is that we live our lives really unaware

19

of what is around us. We *see* lots of things, and we *use* those things—but are we aware? Do we understand the world we see?

Jesus once talked to his disciples about the people in his day who went through their lives unaware. The disciples had asked him why he used parables, or stories, to teach, instead of using good advice and Bible verses.

This is why I speak to them in parables, because seeing they do not see, and hearing they do not hear, nor do they understand. With them indeed is fulfilled the prophecy of Isaiah which says:

"You shall indeed hear but never understand, and you shall indeed see but never perceive. For this people's heart has grown dull, and their ears are heavy of hearing, and their eyes have closed, lest they should perceive with their eyes, and hear with their ears, and understand with their heart and turn for me to heal them."

But blessed are your eyes, for they see, and your ears, for they hear. (Matt. 13:13-16.)

Jesus urged his followers then—and it goes for us now, too—to use their eyes and ears to enable them *really* to understand what is good and true and important in the world. Why should we grope around for the truth, as if we could not see, when God has given us gifts of sight and hearing—and has given us his love to encourage us to get acquainted with the world around us?

Father, help me see the truth, and hear it too, so that I may go through my life aware of the beauty and power of thy world, the work of thy hands. In Jesus' name. AMEN.

you keep looking for ...

The Key to Your Puzzle

JIGSAW PUZZLES AREN'T REALLY HARD TO WORK—IF you can just find the right piece at the right time. The right piece seems to open up the whole solution, and other pieces suddenly fall into place. The problem is not in finding *all* the pieces, but in finding the *key* piece.

And the puzzle you struggle with all your life— yourself—works the same way.

The key is the commitment you make: your big decision, your basic decision that shapes your faith, is your love for God and your gratitude for his love for you. For the key piece of your life, your commitment to accept God's love for you and to begin to live for

21

him, is a first step that helps make sense of all the other decisions that follow it. It is a first step that must be taken by you, and only you can decide to take it.

Have I really committed myself to God, accepting his love for me and returning it to those around me?

Can I offer myself right now, making the big choice that will make sense out of all the puzzling demands on me?

Each person finds his own answer to these questions —and all of us do not express our answer in the same ways. One expression of the big choice was made by Jesus, in these words:

Therefore do not be anxious, saying, "What shall we eat?" or "What shall we drink?" or "What shall we wear?" For the Gentiles seek all these things, and your heavenly Father knows that you need them all. But seek first his kingdom and his righteousness, and all these things shall be yours as well. (Matt. 6:31-33.)

These words might help you express in your own way the commitment you want to make. If you have not already made that commitment, would you like to make it now?

Help me, O God, to find ways to thank you for your love. I want to give myself to you. In Jesus' name I pray. AMEN.

You're Not a Slot Machine

EVER PUT A PENNY IN THE SCALES AND GET A LITTLE card with your weight and your fortune on it? That's just one of the many things you can get from a coin machine these days. Do you need change? or a cup of hot chocolate? or a cold drink? or a book? a special song? or something else? All you have to do is put a coin in the slot, press the button, and presto! Out it comes.

Wouldn't it be nice if you could get the answers to your problems that way—instant decisions? You wouldn't have to stop and ask yourself if this or that is the right thing to do. You wouldn't have to worry about what your friends will think of you if you don't go along with the crowd. You wouldn't have to be bothered about what this will mean for your parents, or your schoolwork, or for your own future. You wouldn't be constantly annoyed by that silly conscience. All your decisions would be made for you.

But you are not a slot machine. Thank goodness for that! Each of us has a mind, and it is up to us to make decisions. Sometimes we don't make very good use of our minds—we let others do our thinking for us and we just go along. And sometimes when we do think a question through and come out with an answer that we feel is right, we push it aside because we think our friends might not agree, or because we are afraid we will look foolish to them. Or, maybe we just don't want to follow through—we think it will be more fun if we just forget what we know is the right thing to do.

In any case, decision-making isn't easy, and sometimes we really do wish we could put a penny in the slot and have the right decision handed out to us. But there are some helps for us in making decisions:

1. We can really try to get the *facts*—not just what "they say" or what we think.

2. We can ask an adult friend or a parent to think through our problems with us.

3. We can turn to our Bibles for guidance.

4. We can pray about it.

5. We can hold up on making a decision (usually this is possible) until we have thought through to some sound conclusion.

Perhaps you will want to add your own prayer today to that of the psalmist:

Make me to know thy ways, O Lord;
  teach me thy paths.
Lead me in thy truth, and teach me. (Ps. 25:4-5a.)

when you find God real . . .

Obey Your Vision

HAVE YOU EVER WISHED FOR A VISION OF GOD—A moment that would show you exactly who God is and just what he expects of you?

To many persons—especially in the past—God's truth has been revealed in a moment of flashing glory. From that time forward their lives were shaped by the vision they had seen. The vision of God came in a sudden and overpowering flash of light to Paul as he was on his way to Damascus to persecute the people of God —and from then on Paul was a new man, dedicated to doing God's work in the world.

But such unusual and earthshaking visions come to very few of the followers of Christ. And yet all of us wish God would come to us so clearly and unmistakably that we would know we had met him.

How does God speak to us, if not in flashing lights or roaring winds?

Sometimes he speaks through the people around us. After all, he has placed them around us, and we are not surprised to find that he is speaking to us through them. Paul's vision came very soon after he had seen

25

Stephen, a Christian, stoned to death—and the haunting memory of the death of that good man no doubt led Paul to open himself to the vision from God on the Damascus Road.

Sometimes God speaks through events that happen around us. Sometimes when the whole world around us seems to have lost its senses, God's quiet voice speaks to us, and we can find order and peace in surroundings that seem to be spinning crazily toward destruction. The Old Testament prophets found God's will in the events of history, and often warned the people that their failures and defeats were the result of God's actions in the world around them, the result of their rejection of God.

Sometimes God's voice speaks clearly to us when we are using our minds to seek out the truths of the world. Suddenly we know that out of all our thinking and wondering, and in the midst of our search, he has spoken, and we know that he has plans for us and that we must get to work on them.

But most important of all is what we do when, in God's own good time, he speaks to us clearly and meaningfully. Paul reported to one of the rulers of his day about his experience on the way to Damascus.

"O King Agrippa, I was not disobedient to the heavenly vision." (Acts 26:19.)

26

Now you are eager to know God's will for your life. You must be willing to seek—but also to wait. Some-day you will know. The vision will come to you in the way God has planned. When it comes—will you be obedient to it?

Our Father, I thank you that I can know about you through the Bible and through Christ. Help me prepare to hear you whenever you speak to me and show me your plan for my life. AMEN.

maybe it will be . . .

Only a Temporary Job!

BETTY HAS A BABY-SITTING BUSINESS LINED UP FOR the summer. Tom has a part-time job as delivery boy for the neighborhood grocery. Ellen is going to take telephone calls for her father in his office. Her brother is going to take over Ken's paper route while Ken is away at camp.

Each of these young people has a different motive for working this summer. Betty wants to earn money for some new school clothes for next year. Tom wants to buy a new camera—he's a shutterbug. Ellen thinks she will be bored with nothing to do and just wants to be busy. Her brother is taking Ken's paper route to help his friend hold his job.

As soon as these teenagers go to work, they will find that their jobs have certain drawbacks. First, there's the time a job takes. You can't do your work and at the same time go swimming, or telephone your friends, or just laze about the house. And you have to be punctual. You can't just go to work any old time you get ready—there are certain hours you must work. And there is the matter of finishing up, too. Most jobs require a certain amount of work each day. You can't just leave the part you don't like and go on to something else you'd rather do. Whether you like it or not, the work is there to be done and done at a certain time.

When we decide that we would like to get a job for the summer, or during holiday vacations, or on weekends, whatever our motive may be, we have to consider all of these points. We have to decide which is more important for us—getting a job or having the time for ourselves. And we have to ask ourselves if we are willing to give up some of the things we'd rather do.

If you are thinking about trying to get a part-time job, ask yourself: Am I grown-up enough to do the job regularly and cheerfully without feeling sorry for myself because I have to give up some fun things? Am

I willing to see it through—to do a good job each day and finish what I have agreed to do?

Knowing that we have done our best and have completed a task is one of the most important rewards that can come from any work—whether it is a part-time job outside the home or some of the work of the family at home. Being willing to accept the demands of a task and make the changes in our habits that are necessary for completing it is a sign that we are indeed becoming more mature, that we are indeed growing up.

For we are fellow workmen for God. (1 Cor. 3:9a.)

O God, guide and strengthen me as I try to become adult in my attitudes toward work. Remind me often that I am working with thee, no matter what the task may be—no matter if it is only a temporary job. And help me pause often to examine my motives in working, to make sure that I am placing value on the right things. AMEN.

But I Want to Be Free

"MY PARENTS WANT TO RUN MY LIFE," SAYS TOM. "I don't really have anything to say about what I do, or where I go, or who I go with. They want to make all my decisions for me. I wish I could be free—free to go where I want to go and free to do what I want to do."

Right next door another teenager is telling her best friend, "Sometimes I'm afraid. I think about my parents dying and me being left all alone. It frightens me. Who will love me then? I'm not pretty—will anyone ever want to marry me? I wish I could be free —free of this fear of being alone and not being loved."

And one of their friends is saying to his teacher, "I would like to be a teacher when I finish school—a special kind of teacher who works with handicapped children. But my parents object. My father says I have to go into his business and carry on the family tradition. I wish I could be free—free to choose what I want to do."

Each of these teenagers wants to be free—in a different way. Do you, too, sometimes feel that you are not free—that you are not being allowed to live your own life, or that you are trapped by fear, guilt, or bad habits?

You can be free, you know. But perhaps not in just the way you have been thinking about it. For freedom is not just doing what we want to do—real freedom comes from the feelings inside ourselves. And we learn to be free as we learn to handle our feelings—even about being "run" by others.

So Jesus said . . . "If you are faithful to what I have said, you are truly my disciples. And you will know the truth and the truth will set you free!" (John 8:31-32, Phillips.)

As we grow in our understanding of what Jesus' life and teaching mean, as we learn to see ourselves and others as God's children, made "in his image," then truth begins to open up to us. We begin to see things in a clearer light, to understand why people speak and act as they do, to judge our own actions by a different set of standards.

When you look at a drop of rain, you see only a small globule of water. But if you put that drop of rain under a microscope, a whole new world of shape, color, and activity opens up to you. So it is when we apply the teachings of Jesus in our lives. Truth opens up to us and frees us in spirit.

31

We do not come by this freedom overnight. But the more we work at it; the more we study; the more we keep on trying; the more we become aware that the old fears, the old guilt, the old sense of being trapped that used to bother us begin to disappear—then we will be free in spirit.

O God, remind me often to turn to thee when I feel trapped by the domination of others, by my own fears, or by my own stupid blunderings. Sharpen my mind to discover the truth about each problem, and guide me in using that truth to grow as a person who is really free. Amen.

when you wonder . . .

Who Is Jesus Christ?

IN A NEW YORK SUBWAY ENTRANCE TWO RUNNING men bumped into a small newsboy and knocked him down. His papers scooted out over the subway platform. One of the men pushed the boy out of his way and trampled over the spilled papers to catch his train. But the other one stopped to help the boy up. He brushed him off and was helping him pick up his papers when he was surprised with a question: "Who are you, mister —Jesus?"

The newsboy knew just enough about Jesus to know that his unknown helper was acting like he had heard Jesus would act. But he was confused, as many of us are. All our lives we've heard about Jesus Christ, and many of us are not sure of all we have heard. Was Jesus a good man, and nothing else? Why do we call him God's Son? If he rose from the dead, why can't *we* see him? And why does the preacher sometimes pray to him, as if he were God?

One of Jesus' early followers tells us who he thought Jesus was. Using the language of his day, he calls Jesus the "Word" that God spoke to the world. Listen to what he says:

In the beginning was the Word, and the Word was with God, and the Word was God. He was in the beginning with God; all things were made through him, and without him was not anything made that was made. In him was life, and the life was the light of men. The light shines in the darkness, and the darkness has not overcome it. (John 1:1-5.)

And then he continues about the coming of the Word.

33

And the Word became flesh and dwelt among us, full of grace and truth; we have beheld his glory, glory as of the only Son from the Father. . . . And from his fulness have we all received, grace upon grace. For the law was given through Moses; grace and truth came through Jesus Christ. No one has ever seen God; the only Son, who is in the bosom of the Father, he has made him known. (John 1:14, 16-18.)

So John says that *Jesus is God's Son who came to the world to make God known.* Throughout all the years of history on the earth God tried to show man his love —but only when he came to earth himself, in the form of his Son, did we realize who he was, and accept his love for us.

Not that we accepted him at first. The first people to whom Christ came killed him; they were upset over what he said about them (that they were evil) and about God (that God loved them anyway). But Christ did not stay dead. First thing anyone knew, he was present in the world, even as he is today, speaking to men's hearts, showing what God is like.

I thank thee, God, for thy Son, Jesus Christ. Help me to learn more about him by reading about him and by seeking to do his will. I want to follow him. I need you to give me strength to become his disciple. In his name I pray. AMEN.

you keep wondering . . .

What Am I Going to Be?

THE WORDS OF THIS MEXICAN PRAYER REMIND US OF
what we are *not*:

> I am only a spark,
>   *Make me a fire.*
> I am only a string,
>   *Make me a lyre.*
> I am only a drop,
>   *Make me a fountain.*
> I am only an ant hill,
>   *Make me a mountain.*
> I am only a feather,
>   *Make me a wing.*
> I am only a rag,
>   *Make me a king.*[1]

Most of our lives are spent in *becoming* something
we are not. When we are babies, everything that happens to us helps us reach the next stage in life—childhood. And all of childhood's years work together to
move us on into adulthood. And every adult moment is
spent in changing from what we are *now* to what we
will be.

Right now, who am I? Why are so many happy days followed by crazy, tough days that don't seem to make sense? What things mean the most to me? I know I'm not the person my friends think I am—I wonder sometimes whether I'm even the person *I* think I am.

I know for sure I'm not the person I want to be. The spark in me needs fanning into a flame. Instead of being a feather, I want to become a wing, flying ahead, finding a way through the sky toward—toward what?

I wish I knew, but I don't.

No one knows—but this much you can be sure of: today's moments are *becoming-moments.* As you reflect on what you are now and what you want to be, God's enfolding love is moving through your efforts and your actions, turning sparks into flames that won't be bright until tomorrow, turning feathers into wings that won't soar for many days to come. But when you have faith that today's becoming-moments are being molded by your hopes and God's plans, you can wait to see what lies ahead. Remember:

A man's mind plans his way, but the Lord directs his steps. (Prov. 16:9.)

Our Father, what is in store for me? Are there days ahead that will make my fretting today seem foolish? Help me learn to wait patiently to find out what I shall become. In Jesus' name. AMEN.

36

on second thought . . .

I May Be a Snob

HAVE YOU EVER HEARD REMARKS SOMETHING LIKE these? "I don't like her looks." "He's not our kind." "Their parents don't amount to much." "What could you expect? His grandfather was a common ditch-digger."

Whenever anyone makes such a remark, he is telling us more about himself than he is telling us about the other person.

He is telling us that he has very little respect for persons. He is telling us that appearances mean more to him than persons do. He is telling us that he is conceited, that he considers himself superior to another person—in short, that he's a snob.

Furthermore, a person who makes such remarks is telling us that he is forgetting Jesus' teachings about the worth of each person in God's creation.

No one was ridiculed; no one was turned away by Jesus. He welcomed the children, the old people, the lepers, the poor and the rich, the good people and the sinners, whoever was ill or in trouble. He did not judge them but tried to help them, and was often so completely exhausted that he had to get away for a time of prayer and rest before he could continue ministering to them.

Doesn't Jesus' acceptance of all people force us— if we are really serious about this business of being a Christian—to ask: Do I accept people as they are? Do I try to find out what they are really like? Or do I judge them by the standards of my crowd? my club? my neighborhood?

Love is patient and kind; love is not jealous or boastful; it is not arrogant or rude. . . . It is not irritable or resentful. . . . Make love your aim. (I Cor. 13:4-5; 14:1*a*.)

O God, forgive me for the times I have made thoughtless remarks about another person. Forgive me, too, for the times I have unthinkingly accepted the prejudices of individuals or groups and parroted what they have said. Help me learn to accept persons for what they are and to see each one as a person of dignity and worth —as Jesus did. AMEN.

God's Gifts, and Yours

WHEN GEORGE WASHINGTON CARVER HAD FINISHED HIS education and was ready to begin his life as a scientist and educator, he said to God, "God, tell me the secrets of the universe."

But God replied, "George, that knowledge is for me alone."

So he tried again, "God, tell me the mystery of the peanut."

And now God's answer was different: "Well, George, that's more nearly your size—I'll do it."

Dr. Carver did not hesitate to ask for a big gift. But he was wise enough to know that even a small gift from God could be of great worth. He took the information he had and spent most of his life studying the peanut, until he had finally developed over three hundred products he could make from it—soap, ink, and even a coffee substitute!

God's gifts to us usually come in sizes we can handle. His greatest gift, his own love for us, no matter whether or not we deserve it, overwhelms us. And yet, by simply

39

accepting that love we become a channel through which his love can move to other people around us.

And what about our gifts to God? We make an offering at church, and sometimes we take part in special sacrificial projects to further the work of the church. But we all know that these gifts are not the gift God really wants. They simply serve as symbols of the gift he is after.

What gift does he want?

Jesus helps us understand the gift God wants from us, our very lives. Remember what he told his disciples?

If any man would come after me, let him deny himself and take up his cross and follow me. For whoever would save his life will lose it, and whoever loses his life for my sake will find it. For what will it profit a man, if he gains the whole world and forfeits his life? Or what shall a man give in return for his life? (Matt. 16:24-26.)

The apostle Paul reminded his friends in Corinth that God's Spirit is with them to help them understand the many gifts God offers them:

Now we have received not the spirit of the world, but the Spirit which is from God, that we might understand the gifts bestowed on us by God. (I Cor. 2:12.)

God offers us many surprising gifts, all of them gifts that we can accept and use as we work in the

40

world. And when we offer him our gifts—and the very special gift of ourselves—he hands us back the biggest gift of all: he lets us serve him.

Pray that God will accept your gift of yourself. And ask him to give you gifts that will help you spend your life serving people around you.

in this world of influences . . .

Who Makes up Your Mind?

It all started with talk.

Without talk civilization would be right where it was before that unrecorded day when our grunting, stone-wielding ancestors discovered the spoken word. With this new magic they could carry their past with them and remember their plans and carry them out.

And for centuries talk was our main means of communicating. Writing and reading came along after many generations had passed. And then—in our own century—there came a revolution, a revolution we are taking part in whether we want to or not. For the first time in history we have miraculous channels of communication that can put every corner of the earth in close,

41

constant contact with every other corner. We can know almost instantaneously about the passage of a new law that will affect our future. We can know—as soon as a candidate himself knows—who has won an election. We can actually witness history taking place thousands of miles away—as a new concert artist plays his first sonata for the entire nation or as a president's assassin is murdered before our very eyes.

The new channels of communication have changed the whole world we live in. They have unmeasured influence on us and sometimes even do our thinking for us in ways we are not aware of.

What do we do about this revolution going on around us? As a Christian, what do you do about the power being turned loose in the world?

For one thing: You can decide not to soak up any and every message coming to you through the newspaper or radio or television. You can pick and choose and evaluate.

But don't forget: When you begin screening out messages that seem false, you don't want to refuse to listen to the viewpoints of persons who disagree with you. *Listening* to a phony message is one thing; *swallowing* it is another!

Also: The TV set can easily become a substitute personality for you, if you surrender to it. You can decide not to be hypnotized by the mass means of communication, remembering to save time for creative and meditative moments alone and with friends.

Once Paul was afraid his friends in Rome were going to be overpowered by the messages of the world around them. Listen to what he wrote to them:

I appeal to you therefore, brethren, by the mercies of God, to present your bodies as a living sacrifice, holy and acceptable to God, which is your spiritual worship. Do not be conformed to this world but be transformed by the renewal of your mind, that you may prove what is the will of God, what is good and acceptable and perfect. (Rom. 12:1-2.)

O God, help me open my life to the world around me, and show me ways to let the world's true messages renew my mind and transform me into the person you are calling me to be. In Christ's name. AMEN.

check yourself on . . .

Sharing Responsibility

EACH MEMBER OF JUDY'S FAMILY HAD AGREED TO HELP with the dishwashing after the evening meal. They worked out a schedule, and each person knew just when to plan for his turn at the dishwashing detail.

But on Judy's night the schedule never seemed to work. Sometimes she would beg off, saying she had a mountain of homework to do—that tomorrow was the last day for that term paper or she might flunk the test tomorrow if she didn't cram tonight. Sometimes she would talk with her friends on the telephone—on and on until her mother or her older sister almost had the dishes finished. Sometimes she would just sit down and watch TV, and then the whole family would get into an argument because she was not doing her share of the family's work.

It's easy to see that Judy was not growing up very fast. In fact, she was being pretty childish. She was not accepting her share of responsibility for the work of the family, nor was she following up on the agreement that had been reached by all members of the family.

True, washing dishes isn't the most pleasant task in the world. But as we become adults, we learn that there are many responsibilities we must assume which are not just exactly to our liking. And when we learn to do what has to be done or what we have agreed to do, cheerfully, without trying to get out of it, then we are really growing up.

Am I doing my share of the work in my home? Are there some tasks that I ought to be responsible for? Do I do my work at home regularly, cheerfully, and on time, without having to be reminded? Could I do anything about dividing up the work in our family so that things can move more smoothly?

Do your best to present yourself to God as one approved, a workman who has no need to be ashamed. (II Tim. 2:15a.)

Father, help me learn to accept my share of responsibility in my home. Forgive me when I forget and lapse into childish behavior, and show me how to do better next time. AMEN.

when you wonder what it means to be . . .

Pure in Heart

THEY SAY JOHN KEATE, THE ENGLISH SCHOOLMASTER, had a stern way with the boys he taught. Every day he greeted them with the challenge: "Be pure in heart, lads, or I'll flog you!"

No doubt his "lads" worked hard to see to it that Keate never *saw* them when they were not as "pure in heart" as he had ordered them to be—but chances are his threat did very little to help them escape the temptations that face all schoolboys.

45

When Jesus was describing persons who were the followers of God's way, one of the phrases he used was this beatitude:

Blessed are the pure in heart, for they shall see God. (Matt. 5:8.)

If Jesus meant by that what Keate meant, there is not much hope for any of us! For who among all of us can claim never to have been tempted to walk in ways that are not good? To be pure in heart means something else than to be free from temptation. Many other of Jesus' teachings give us an idea of what he meant:

Seek first his kingdom and his righteousness. . . .
He who loves father or mother more than me is not worthy of me; and he who loves son or daughter more than me is not worthy of me. . . .
The kingdom of heaven is like a merchant in search of fine pearls, who, on finding one pearl of great value, went and sold all that he had and bought it. (Matt. 6:33a; 10:37; 13:45-46.)

The person who is pure in heart, you see, is one whose heart has one main purpose that is never turned aside by other purposes. A "pure" heart does not escape temptations; it meets its full share of temptations. But it meets them with one pure goal: to meet temptation head-on and subdue it by the power of God's love.

No indeed—being "pure in heart" does not mean you

46

will be able to avoid impure thoughts and wishes. *It does mean that once you commit yourself to living Christ's way, your heart seeks to have one single, un-wavering purpose: to serve God and to do his will.*

You know even better than I do, God, the many temptations I meet. Help me remain pure and steadfast in my loyalty to you. Forgive me when my utmost effort fails—and I have to remember how weak I am and how much I need your strong love. In Jesus' name. AMEN.

there's more to it than . . .

Daydreaming

> Would you like to swing on a star?
> Carry moonbeams home in a jar?
> Or be better off than you are?
> Or . . .²

IT ISN'T HARD TO UNDERSTAND WHY THIS WAS A POPU-lar song a few years ago. In addition to the lilting melody, we are intrigued by the fantasy. In imagination we are free—gaily swinging out among the stars, capturing the golden beauty of moonbeams. And of course none of us would object to being better off than we are!

Yes, it's fun to lose ourselves in a world of fantasy, to set our imaginations free to wander, to make wishes about what we want to do and what we want to have and what we want to be.

But we don't become what we want to become, get what we want, or do what we want to do merely by dreaming and wishing. Anyone knows better than that. It takes some real thought and effort to make a dream come true. And we have to test our dreams, ask ourselves such questions as:

Is it really possible to make this dream come true? If this dream can be made to come true, will I be a better person? Will other persons be happier or better off? Or would my dream coming true shatter someone else's dreams?

If we are reasonably certain that our dreams are good dreams, then we need to begin working right now to make them come true.

In the Bible there is a story of a young king who asked God for something in a dream. He asked:

Give thy servant therefore an understanding mind . . . that I may discern between good and evil. (I Kings 3:9a.)

In your prayer today perhaps you will want to ask God for an "understanding mind" so that you can make your dreams come true.

Finding Your Place

A CIVIL WAR SOLDIER WAS GROPING HIS WAY THROUGH the line of battle, looking for a commanding officer. He was obviously lost, dazed by the noise and pressure and danger. At last he found a captain and asked the officer to assign him to a regiment. The captain just waved his hand in a sweeping motion, pointing to the entire battlefield. "Fall in anywhere, soldier. There's good fighting all along the line."

When it comes to finding the right spot in life, there's good fighting all along the line, too. Contrary to what many young people think, there is not just one special job cut out for each of us that we spend our lives looking for. That's a romantic notion, of course, and lots of fancy stories have been written about the good guys and the bad guys: those who found their one right spot in life and those who didn't.

But a Christian knows that he is being called to a world that is in need of his service. And the need is so great that there are many places where each person can fall in and do his part.

Then how do you know what you should do, if you

don't wait to find your own special niche that has been chosen for you?

First of all, you decide to do the job that needs doing closest at hand—like the good Samaritan did. He wasn't a doctor, after all. But he knew when he was needed, and he wasn't afraid to help.

Second, you decide to find a job that will let you make the most of the talents and abilities God has given you. You don't just choose a job you *like*—you look for the kind of job that will challenge you and let you make a contribution.

Most important, you make up your mind that the job you do is being done for one main reason: to express your gratitude to God for loving you. He has given you life and shown you how to find life's meaning. He has given you gifts and opportunities to use them. In turn, you say "thank you" by getting to work and helping other people around you find out what kind of God there is in the world: a loving Father who has gifts for them too.

This is my commandment, that you love one another as I have loved you. Greater love has no man than this, that a man lay down his life for his friends. You are my friends if you do what I command you. No longer do I call you servants, for the servant does not know what his master is doing; but I have called you friends, for all that I have heard from my Father I have made known to you. You did not choose me, but I chose you and appointed you that you should go and bear fruit and that your fruit should abide; so that whatever you ask the Father in my name, he may give it to you. This I command you, to love one another. (John 15: 12-17.)

Since you have chosen me, God, help me choose wisely the spot from which I can serve thee all my life. I pray in Jesus' name. AMEN.

when you wonder what to do . . .

About Brothers and Sisters

DO YOU HAVE YOUNGER BROTHERS OR SISTERS? IF SO, how do you get along with them?

It isn't always easy to put up with the noisiness and nosiness of younger children. We know that the things we are doing are important, and we get very upset when they ask questions and interfere in our affairs. Sometimes, too, we are embarrassed by what they say and do—particularly when our friends are present. And sometimes—let's face it—we may be just a bit jealous when they "steal the show."

51

But how about our own behavior? How do we treat these members of our family who are younger? Learning to get along with others is not limited to our own age group, you know. As long as we live, in our work and in our homes, wherever we are and whatever we are doing, we will be coming in contact with younger persons. A part of our growing up is learning to get along with them. There is no better place to begin than in our own homes. Right now we can begin to find ways to grow in understanding younger persons and in discovering ways to get along with them.

Think about these questions today: Could it be that I am a little selfish, so occupied with my own interests that I do not try to get along? Could it be that sometimes when brothers and sisters annoy me they are just as troubled as I am?

You may remember that the disciples were once quite upset because the children were crowding about Jesus. How embarrassed they must have been by what he told them! Is there any teaching for us here?

Then some people came to him bringing little children for him to touch. The disciples tried to discourage them. When Jesus saw this, he was indignant and told them: "You must let little children come to me—never stop them! For the kingdom of God belongs to such as these. Indeed, I assure you that the man who does not accept

52

the kingdom of God like a little child will never enter it."

Then he took the children in his arms and laid his hands on them and blessed them. (Mark 10:13-16, Phillips.)

Our Father, I realize that I have a long way to go in being truly Christian—especially in relationships with younger persons in my family. Help me control my temper, learn to speak without anger. Show me new ways to avoid conflict and hurt feelings. AMEN.

it's a different kind of fun . . .

When You Are Alone

GOING SWIMMING WITH THE CROWD IS LOTS OF FUN. All the splashing and shouting and stunting add up to a fine time. But then, for just a few minutes you drift away. You float on your back and look at the green lace of leaves against the sky. Or you just leisurely tread water and watch the silver ripples. That's fun, too—a different kind of fun.

And in the winter it's great sport to go whizzing down the hill on a bobsled loaded down with laughing friends. But it's fun, too, to sit quietly in a sleigh listening to the soft thud-thud of the horses' hooves and the crisp tinkle of sleighbells as you skim along in the moonlight.

It's good to be with our friends—to laugh and talk together. And sometimes we like to lose ourselves in a crowd and let the excitement take us over. But there are times when we need to be alone, too. We need time to think, to make decisions, to plan, and just to let our minds go wandering. We can't see the loveliness of the leaf patterns overhead until we get away from the crowd, and the sound of sleighbells can be drowned out with shouts and laughter.

When we are alone, we can see things more clearly. We have the time and quietness in which to appreciate beauty that we have not seen or heard before. In moments away from the rush and excitement we can recall what has been happening in our world of togetherness. We can sort out our feelings about persons and work out decisions. Away from the crowd we can open our minds to new ideas in books, music, and art. We can turn our imaginations loose, adventure with some creative project. Yes, there is joy in being with our families and friends, but there is also a deep joy in learning to be alone. This is a part of growing up, too.

Think about these questions today: Is my life a little lopsided? Do I spend too much time with others? Too much time alone? What can I do about it?

54

For God alone my soul waits in silence;
    from him comes my salvation.
He only is my rock and my salvation,
    my fortress. (Ps. 62:1-2a.)

Today as you pray, ask God to show you how to make good use of your time—how to find time to be alone—how to make the most of time spent with others —and by yourself.

when you ask yourself . . .

Am I a Christian?

WHAT DOES IT MEAN—TO BE A CHRISTIAN?

At first, that word was a nickname. People called the first followers of Christ "the Christ-people," or "little Christs," which is pretty much what the word originally meant. But the nickname stuck (as nicknames usually do), and millions of people in the world today are proud to be called by it.

When we say about ourselves, or about someone we know, that we are Christians, we mean much the same thing the ancient people did who first coined the word for their neighbors who had placed their faith in the man they called Christ. *We mean that we are little Christs.*

That does not mean that we assume that we are as good or as true as Jesus Christ was. It means that we are trying to follow his way and show his way to people we know. We want those around us to be able to see in us something of him. In the way we treat our neighbors, we want them to know that we are following Christ's demand that we love one another. In the way we handle the many things that belong to us, we want to be saying, "Look, I'm using the world around me as a good steward would, as Christ commanded." In making plans and determining values, we try to show that our faith in Christ is helping shape our way of doing things.

So, being a Christian means doing things in a certain style—the style of Christ.

It also means recognizing that we are a part (and only a small part) of a worldwide fellowship. We recognize our need of this fellowship, and we are encouraged to remember that together we make a mighty force seeking to find and do God's will. Each one of us is tiny and ineffective alone. But, just as the millions of tiny, hairy roots of a large oak tree can lift a hundred gallons of water every day to supply the tree with its life fluid, *together we communicate God's love to a thirsty world.*

What do you mean when you say you are a Christian?
You are saying you are Christ's.

You are saying you are trying to style your life after his way of life.

You are saying that you belong to a community of believers whose faith helps them move mountains and show God's love to all men.

Jesus said in the Sermon on the Mount:

Every one then who hears these words of mine and does them will be like a wise man who built his house upon the rock; and the rain fell, and the floods came, and the winds blew and beat upon that house, but it did not fall, because it had been founded on the rock. And every one who hears these words of mine and does not do them will be like a foolish man who built his house upon the sand; and the rain fell and the floods came, and the winds blew and beat against that house, and it fell; and great was the fall of it. (Matt. 7:24-27.)

I am glad, O God, that I am a Christian, a follower of Jesus Christ. Help me increase my faith in you and in him so that I can find ways to show my love to all around me. AMEN.

you can help . . .

When Things Don't Go Right at Home

IN THE HUGE GRANITE QUARRY AT BARRE, VERMONT—
the largest and deepest granite quarry in the world—
the great twenty-ton blocks of granite are lifted to the
surface by derricks. The derricks are driven by electri-
cally powered hoists operated by engineers in hoist-
houses at some distance from the derricks. These engineers take their signals from a signalman who super-
vises the work of the derricks. In turn, he acts on signals
from derrickmen deep down in the quarry. Because they
cannot hear each other above the deafening noise of the
quarrying, these workmen have developed a unique sys-
tem of hand signals. Each one knows exactly what to do
when he gets the signal from a fellow worker even
though they may be hundreds of feet apart. Their signals are all-important. In this highly skilled work that
calls for exact timing, the derrickman can endanger both
himself and the others if he does not know the signals,
if he does not give the proper signals, or if he fails to
follow the signals given.

Sometimes in our relationships with parents we're

like the derrickman in the quarry. We might be able
to get along just fine if only we could follow the signals.
But often we don't know the signals. We don't know
exactly what our parents expect of us. We are uncertain about just what the rules are. And parents may be
just as puzzled—they don't know our signals either.

For example, take the matter of the time you come
home at night. Could it just be that your parents have
a right to feel uneasy when you don't show up on time?
Did you clear on signals before you left so they would
know where you are, who you are with, and approxi-
mately when the party, date, movie, or whatever would
be over? And how about your parents—did they clear
their signals with you—let you know what they thought
was a reasonable hour to come in? If your signals didn't
check, could you have taken time to talk it over and
reach some agreement without becoming angry? True,
things are quite different now than when your parents
were your age, but not so different that you cannot work
out some signals that will work for all concerned.

*Spend some time thinking about plans for the next
few days. Ask: Can I foresee any possibility of misunderstandings with parents about what I will be doing?
If so, what can I do about a set of signals that my
parents can depend on? That I can depend on?*

My son, keep sound wisdom and discretion;
   let them not escape from your sight. . . .
Then you will walk on your way securely
   and your foot will not stumble. (Prov. 3:21, 23.)

Help me, O God, to do my part to prevent misunderstandings with my parents. Slow me down long enough to think out and talk out agreements about the things that can cause trouble between us. In Jesus' name I pray. Amen.

everyday you have to . . .

Keep on Trying

When thomas a. edison, working in America, and J. W. Swan, working in England, came up with the electric light bulb, everyone thought the end had been reached in this kind of experimentation. There was now a safe means of lighting streets and buildings with electricity.

But after a time researchers began to find other uses for the electric light bulb. New types of bulbs were developed for making use of ultraviolet rays and for infrared heat rays. Still others were developed that would kill bacteria in the air, and before long these were produced in numerous styles and sizes for use in hospitals, schools, homes, and even in chicken houses.

These are only a few of the uses discovered for that original electric light bulb. You can think of many more uses, and of course researchers do not stop here; they keep on trying to find new and better ways to make use of the electric light bulb.

We can find something of a parallel here for our lives. Often when we reach one high spot or make a special gain, we feel pretty proud of ourselves. We have it made. And we quit trying.

John is making a C-average in school. "That's O.K.," he says. "I'm just an average person. I can get by on a good old C."

Margaret is making A's. "I worked pretty hard to pull my grades up, but I can relax now," she says.

"I do pretty well in this being-a-Christian business," says Tom. "I go to church and Sunday school. I don't really do anything that's bad."

And so on and so on.

True, each of these teenagers has achieved something, made some progress. But is that all that can be done? Have they made full use of their abilities?

If John is a C-student, chances are that if he just keeps trying, he could go beyond a C. Or at least he

61

would so strengthen that C that it would mean more to him later on.

And Margaret—an A-average isn't the end. Those A's could take a quick tumble if she doesn't continue doing good work. Or if she's a brain and work comes easy, maybe she needs to start working in another direction—doing some interesting reading, developing a hobby or special interest.

And being a Christian—surely Tom doesn't think that going to church and Sunday school and keeping out of trouble is all there is to it? If we are to be true followers of Jesus—and that's what being a Christian means—then we have to keep on trying, day after day, in everything we do. We never actually arrive. We are always seeking—seeking Jesus' teaching for us in each situation, trying to be better than we are.

Like the researchers who work with the electric light bulbs, we have to keep on, even though we sometimes fail and make many mistakes.

In what areas of my life do I need to try harder— in my schoolwork? in my friendships? getting along with my family? How about my relationships with persons of other religions, races, or different social backgrounds?

Never flag in zeal, be aglow with the Spirit, serve the Lord. (Rom. 12:11.)

Help me keep on trying, O God, even when I feel that I have done a good piece of work or have made real progress in the way I am handling my life. Forgive me when I make mistakes and when I give up and quit trying. Strengthen me to start over again, to keep on trying. AMEN.

your time of life can be . . .

A Time for Loving

OF ALL THE EXCITING THINGS THAT HAPPEN TO TEENS the most exciting of all has to do with romance.

Just as your mind has been developing during the first years of your life and your spirit has been deepening as you have met more and more of the world, your body has been growing and developing, too. You are moving along toward the day when all of the signs of childhood and youth are gone, and you will be a young adult, at the peak of life.

The growth of your body has brought with it many puzzling problems, as well as many new and exciting opportunities.

Suddenly, perhaps, you've put on a spurt of growth,

63

and the gym shorts you started the semester with are now long outgrown.

Or your complexion, perhaps, is cutting up and pulling you constantly back to the mirror to fret about the "new" you that you aren't used to yet.

And probably you're familiar by now with a special tingle all over when you brush close to a particular person—the boy or girl who in a very special way appeals to you.

These experiences (and all the others you could add!) are little signs of your new adulthood. Taken together, they mean you are growing up—indeed, that you are well on your way to being grown-up.

Take the matter of romance that we started off talking about. By now you are mature enough—grown-up enough, that is—to begin to think about the days ahead when you will be wanting to choose a life partner, the person with whom you will spend the rest of your life: having a family, sharing interests, looking for ways to be together in serving your community. But along with this new maturity comes some confusion. This awakening love you are experiencing is new to you, and it is therefore a bit frightening. You want to treat it in just the right way—and don't know how.

As you try to learn how, remember this:

Your attraction toward a boy- or girl-friend is natural. God has given each of us the capacity to love.

64

It is good, too, this new experience that you face. It is not only good because it is a gift from God, but also because it enables you to fulfill yourself in the years ahead.

And it is exciting. It will color all the rest of your life. If you dedicate yourself to acting responsibly, taking the road that leads to mature and satisfying love, your life will always be opening up wider and wider to the world, and you will find ways to let God's love flow into your relationship with the one you love.

But from the beginning of creation, "God made them male and female." "For this reason a man shall leave his father and mother and be joined to his wife, and the two shall become one." So they are no longer two but one. What therefore God has joined together, let not man put asunder. (Mark 10:6-9.)

Pray today that God will help you find the way to true love. Ask him to give you the courage not to hold back from the exciting and joyful experience of friendship that can lead you toward the partner of your life.

are you sure . . .

A Funny Thing Happened?

FOR YEARS THE COMEDIAN HAS COME ONSTAGE WITH the familiar line, "A funny thing happened on the way to the theater." Sometimes it's a studio instead of a theater, but this line has become a stock pattern for getting into the first joke.

Sometimes we, too, meet our friends with an account of "a funny thing" that happened. We proceed to tell how we pulled "a fast one" on our parents and got to do something we especially wanted to do. We tell how we got Old So-and-So "in a hole," and everyone laughs. We make a good story out of the joke we played on the teacher in first period.

While we're telling the story and have the attention of our friends, we feel quite superior. Their laughter really builds our ego. But afterward—?

The more you really think about such an incident, the more you keep coming back to the question: Was it really funny? Or was it basically cruel—something that caused another person to be hurt or embarrassed or to feel inferior?

Perhaps you have had someone make fun of you

sometime, or you have been the butt of a cruel trick. It wasn't funny then, was it? In self-defense, or because you felt you should be a good sport, you may have laughed with the others, but deep down inside you were really hurt.

Recall some of the "funny things" that have happened in your crowd. Was anyone hurt? Or embarrassed? Or made to feel that he was a second-class citizen? Whether or not you had any part in such incidents, is there anything you can do now to make up for what happened? How about next time—what will you do then?

Love is not jealous or boastful; it is not arrogant or rude. (I Cor. 13:4b-5a.)

A new commandment I give to you, that you love one another. (John 13:34a.)

Forgive me, Father, for the times I have caused others to be hurt or unhappy by doing what I thought was "a funny thing." Help me grow in my relationships with others, remembering always that each person I meet is one of thy children, just as I am. I pray in Jesus' name. AMEN.

don't think you're individual . . .

When You Make Mistakes

IN A CERTAIN FAMILY, SO THE STORY GOES, THE Thanksgiving Day custom was for each person at the table to tell of something he was particularly thankful for. When her turn came, one little girl said that she was thankful for erasers. Naturally, everyone laughed; and when asked why, she explained that erasers rub out mistakes.

Most of us have plenty of mistakes to rub out. None of us is perfect. Every day is peppered with mistakes —mistakes in what we say, mistakes in doing a piece of work or preparing a paper or reciting in class, mistakes in handling our money, mistakes in judging our friends, and on and on. There's really no end. If we could erase our mistakes, it would certainly take a lot of erasers!

Unfortunately life is not that simple. But there are some things we can do about our mistakes. We can make every possible effort to make right a mistake we have made. Often saying we are sorry to a person we have wronged will help, and many times just a word of explanation as to why we made the mistake will go far. When a mistake is the result of carelessness, doing a task over again may correct it. And we can certainly learn through our mistakes. Having made a mistake, we can learn not to do the same thing again. Instead, we can try doing it another way. For as we learn to sidestep future mistakes, we grow in our understanding of ourselves and others.

Think about your mistakes—the most recent ones. Now ask yourself: Why did I make these mistakes? Is there anything I can do about them now? Have I learned anything from these mistakes?

Have mercy on me, O God, according to thy steadfast love;
according to thy abundant mercy blot out my transgressions. . . .
Create in me a clean heart, O God,
and put a new and right spirit within me.
(Ps. 51:1, 10.)

Like the psalmist, Father, I pray that you will blot out my transgressions—forgive me for the mistakes that I have made. Help me to learn from these mistakes, to grow in understanding and in Christian living. And, wherever possible, show me how to make up for my mistakes—especially those which may have hurt my parents and my friends. AMEN.

69

if you're patient and persistent . . .

You Can Learn to Pray

"NOTHING EVER HAPPENS WHEN I PRAY."

"When I pray I feel just like I'm talking to myself."

"Sometimes I wonder if God even hears what I say."

Most young people have a hard time praying. It is not because prayer is *difficult,* but because it is *different.* It's talking, so we make the mistake of thinking it ought to be just as easy as talking to a friend; but when we try it, it isn't. It's thinking, and we assume it ought to be as easy as thinking up other ideas; but we find it isn't that simple.

The strange truth of the matter is that we do not learn how to pray until we know how to pray! Now, before that stops you, think it over. Like many other things in life, prayer is not satisfying until we have tried and tried to make it work; and then, unexpectedly, we discover we are really praying, that we are sure inside that God is listening. Growing in our faith in Christ and his message of God's love helps us try more effectively, and becoming more effective in our praying helps us grow in our faith.

It is much like walking around outside an old church.

When you look at the windows, they look sooty, hardly clean enough to let light shine through. But when you walk up the front steps of the church and go inside and take a look at the same windows, suddenly you realize that from the inside, things are different. The light shines through the grime, and the windows show forth stories of the glory of God. Until we are "inside" of prayer, it holds back its most happy experiences; and only by practice and persistence can we ever get inside.

Several things help us as we try to learn to pray:

Using the prayers of other people—from the Bible and from devotional books—helps you gain confidence.

Using your own words to phrase short but sincere prayers will encourage you to bring your own personal problems and dreams before God.

Learning to be quiet, without getting fretful—and to be patient, without being demanding—will enable you to relax long enough to unwind and let God's spirit begin to find ways to speak to your heart and mind.

Reading favorite Bible passages and then quietly thinking about what they mean for you can help bring you to the doorstep of God's presence.

Today, ask God to help you learn to meet him sincerely in your prayers, and then (without rushing) pray the prayer Jesus taught:

71

Our Father who art in heaven,
Hallowed be thy name.
Thy kingdom come,
Thy will be done,
　On earth as it is in heaven.
Give us this day our daily bread;
And forgive us our debts,
　As we also have forgiven our debtors;
And lead us not into temptation,
　But deliver us from evil.
For thine is the kingdom and the power
　and the glory, forever. AMEN.

if you have learned to pray . . .

You Can't Do All the Talking

THE DIAL TELEPHONE WAS QUITE A WONDER WHEN IT
was first introduced. People had been used to ringing the
operator and waiting for her to make the connection
with the person being called. Now they had a wonderful
new device—they could dial directly and talk with their
friends.

Today we take the dial telephone very much for
granted. It is a part of our daily life just as much
as hamburgers, washing machines, and stereos. We can

reach for the telephone and dial our friends directly in almost any part of the country. And it will be only a short time until we can dial anywhere in the world—perhaps by the time you read this! In this little instrument we have a means of direct communication in our homes—talking with someone at a distance requires only that we lift the receiver and dial the correct number.

Did it ever occur to you that prayer is something like this? Through prayer we have a means of direct communication with God. But we are the ones who must do the "dialing." That is, we are the ones who must make the start—reach out to God with our minds.

Furthermore, we have to "lift the receiver." That is, we have to be still and listen. Just as you would never hear your friend's voice on the telephone if you did all the talking, so you have to remember that you can't do all the talking to God. You have to listen, too.

Sometimes we don't seem to make connection. It seems that we are not really talking with God, that our prayers don't mean very much. When this happens, perhaps we need to remember the word *with*. Prayer is talking *with* God, not *to* him. And when we talk *with* anyone, we spend part of the time listening.

Sometimes, too, our prayers don't mean much because we can't keep our minds on God and on our prayer. All kinds of thoughts come flooding in—we remember

73

that paper for English class, we wonder what to wear for the party Friday night, we think about a way to tell our parents that we're sorry about not cleaning up our room, and on and on.

It may help some to remember that everyone has this trouble at some time in learning to pray. Learning to pray is not easy for any of us, and many times it seems we are making no progress at all. But little by little, if we really keep trying, we begin to learn how to still our minds, how to seek God's guidance, how to listen for his direction.

Am I trying to learn how to control my mind each day—to be quiet? To keep out thoughts of other things? To keep my mind on what I am praying about and on God?

Ask and it will be given to you. Search and you will find. Knock and the door will be opened for you. The one who asks will always receive; the one who is searching will always find, and the door is opened to the man who knocks. (Matt. 7:7-8, Phillips.)

Teach me to pray, Father. Help me learn to discipline my body and my mind—to be quiet, to wait, to listen. Help me center my thoughts and keep them from wandering. In Jesus' name. AMEN.

when you have trouble . . .

Getting Along at School

WHERE DO YOU SPEND MOST OF YOUR TIME, DAY IN AND day out?

If you are like most other young people in America, you spend about a third of your time sleeping, another third of your time visiting, playing, puttering about— and the other third: *in school.*

In the first years of your life, most of your time was spent at Mom's knee. If you were awake, it's a safe bet your mother was not far out of sight. A little later you began to cut the apron strings, and the neighborhood became your world as you spent more and more time in the yard, alone or with playmates. Then eight or nine years ago you took a big step. You started to school. From that moment, home became only one of the places of influence and interest in your life, and life at school began to take on greater importance for you.

School days serve many good purposes, if you stop to think about them:

You make your first break away from the family when you start to school.

You have a chance at school to try out your own way of doing things.

You meet people who are different, who challenge you to learn to be yourself.

You find your first adult counselors—grown-ups who are not family, but who are interested in you.

Most of all, you have a jumping-off place into your adult life.

All these opportunities place a big responsibility on you to get the most out of your school days.

Are you finding ways to help other students who might need your help?

Are you willing to let others lead you when their experience and wisdom surpasses yours?

Are you trying to find ways to grow in your respect for those at school who disagree with you—about politics—about religion—about what life is all about?

Are you trying to be the genuine you, always being yourself so that your teachers and classmates will know that you are trustworthy, capable of becoming a good friend?

If you are growing in these ways, you are learning to let your faith express itself in the things you are doing every day. Set your own goals high, so that you can assume the responsibility that is yours in your school days. *And make this your prayer as you dedicate yourself again:*

Search me, O God, and know my heart!
Try me and know my thoughts! (Ps. 139:23.)

it's not easy to face . . .

The Loss of a Loved One

LOSING A LOVED ONE IS A MAJOR CRISIS IN ANY PERSON'S life. Whether it is a member of the family or a friend, the relationship is cut off sharply and finally by the event of death.

It is particularly difficult to come to terms with death when we are young. Life is so full, so exciting. There is so much to learn, so much to be done, so many experiences waiting for us that it is hard to stop and face the cold reality of death.

Sometimes we burst out with "Why did God do this to me?" We are angry with him because we feel so unhappy and alone. We blame him for breaking into the pattern of our lives, making it necessary for us to find new ways of getting along without the one who has died.

If we are really honest with ourselves, however, and if we are honest about God, we have to admit that:

1. *Death is the natural end of life for all living things in God's creation.* Plants grow, bloom, and die. Animals are born, grow to maturity, bear their young, and die. Man, too, lives by this law of death. When his body wears out, he dies.

2. *Death does not always come in old age after a full life.* There are many unforeseen causes of death—accidents, disease, earthquakes, fires, wars—any number of things. In nature, too, there is the unpredictable cause of death—animals are killed by the hunter or by other animals, by forest fires, by accidents and disease. Trees go down to their death before the great winds, the sweeping fires, or the roaring floodwaters.

3. *God does not single out one person for punishment and take a loved one from him.* God's laws of life and death are established for *all* of his creation. Today you lose a dear friend. Tomorrow a friend loses his parents. And each of us will most certainly die at some time in the future. This is in accord with God's laws.

But even though we accept all of this with our minds, the terrible sense of loss is still there. We still feel grief. This is where our Christian faith helps us. For we know that even though God's own son, Jesus Christ, was killed by his enemies, he was raised up from death. He entered into the hearts of all who loved him. And ever since that first Easter morning, his followers down through the ages have believed that they, too, will live again, even though their bodies die. So even in our grief and loss we can rejoice in the hope that, like Christ, all of us shall live.

Today, as you try to sort out your ideas and your feelings about death, remember that God is with you, "closer than breathing." Open your mind to him—let his Spirit speak. Thank God for Jesus Christ—for the hope that he has given us through his death upon the cross—for the love that fills our lives today—and through all of life that has no end.

for a day when you're . . .

Just an Old Crab

A GROUCHY SAILOR STOMPED HIS WAY INTO A RESTAURANT on the seashore; and as soon as the busy waitress came to his table, he demanded to know, "Do you serve crabs in this place?" She answered him straightaway, "Why, sure, mister—and we'll even serve *you!*"

But she probably wished she didn't have to, for nobody enjoys being around the kind of person we call "crabby." Often as not, he is short-tempered, mad at the world, and full of complaints.

Sometimes the crabby persons we bump into during the day (or discover some mornings when we look into the mirror) have lots of good reasons to be at outs with the world. But the person who is trying to find ways to be friendly and helpful is constantly trying to stay on an even keel in his relationship to people around him. No matter how hard we try, though, there are slipups. Even our best intentions are tripped; and first thing we know, our temper is off and running, and we are desperately embarrassed and disappointed in our failure to remain the kind of person we want to be.

Emotions constantly play tricks on us. And teen-aged boys and girls especially are apt to get tangled up in many confusing feelings—all of them demanding equal time in your day. What can you do?

Realize that the next few years are very important in your life. You will be learning how to live in the world as a young adult—and that explains why there are so many frustrating feelings moving inside you. Your body and mind are having to develop at full speed—and yet your feelings tell you you don't really want to grow up yet. Some days you feel like the funny donkey who wanted to eat oats and drink water at the same time. He never could make up his mind which one he wanted first and never got either one.

As you try to live each day without too much turmoil —keeping your temper, remembering not to be critical of those who love you, smiling whenever you can— remember these words from the New Testament:

Finally all of you, have unity of spirit, sympathy, love of the brethren, a tender heart and a humble mind. Do not return evil for evil or reviling for reviling; but on the contrary bless, for to this you have been called, that you may obtain a blessing. For
"He that would love life and see good days,
let him keep his tongue from evil
and his lips from speaking guile;
let him turn away from evil and do right;
let him seek peace and pursue it." (1 Pet. 3:8-11.)

O God, my Father, help me remain true to myself and to you in these strange days when my temper runs away with me and I cause those I love to be unhappy. Help me understand myself, so I can learn how to show my love for those around me. In Jesus' name. AMEN.

81

you can do something about it . . .

When Your Conscience Hurts

THE WORD "SIN" IS AN UGLY WORD. WE DON'T LIKE IT, and we don't use it very much. In fact, we usually just try to forget it. Yet many of us go to bed at night with troubled consciences. Although we don't actually say the word to ourselves, we feel guilty. We have given in to some temptation. Deep down inside we know we have sinned.

We are not alone in this, of course. All through the ages the prophets, preachers, and teachers have been reminding people of their sinfulness, calling on them to repent and to turn to God. They have pointed out that sin is a deliberate turning away from God, a decision to do something that we know is contrary to the understanding of what God wants us to do.

We know when we are sinning. We are smart enough to know what is right and what is wrong. We are smart enough to realize that we are not behaving as God wants us to. But sometimes we talk ourselves into believing that it's okay to do something wrong—just this once. We push the matters of sin and of God's will to the back of our minds. Afterward we cannot hide behind our own arguments. The fact of right and wrong—the fact of God's will—is there. We know we are being judged by him. And so we become conscience-stricken. We feel guilty and ashamed.

The one thing that we can do that will free us from our guilt is to confess our sin fully and honestly to God. We must hide nothing from him and, if we are truly sorry, ask his forgiveness. Sometimes we also need to ask the forgiveness of a person we have wronged, but more often it is a matter between ourselves and God. We confess our sins and let God know that we are sorry; God's forgiveness lifts our guilt and leaves us free again to try to live according to his will—to sin no more. And if we really try from that time on to obey God's laws and continue trying to discover his will for us, then we can depend on him to strengthen us and help us hold out against temptation when it comes.

If you feel guilty about something you have done recently, perhaps you need to spend some time now in confession, repentance, and prayer for God's guidance in the future.

**God is our refuge and our strength,
a very present help in trouble. (Ps. 46:1.)**

We are all guilty, O God, of forgetting your love and your expectations of us. Forgive us our sins each day

83

—the little sins that we hardly notice and the ugly black sins that weigh us down with guilt. We know that we can do better—that we can be better. Help us put our sins behind us and grow each day in living a life that is patterned after that of thy Son, Jesus Christ. AMEN.

you can't get away with . . .

Fooling Yourself

THE EASIEST PERSON IN THE WORLD TO FOOL IS YOU! Stop and count the ways you fool yourself:

not admitting your mistakes
pretending you can do things you know you can't
putting blame where it doesn't belong
claiming you don't need to study.

Covering up our goofs is a childish way of getting around problems. Unfortunately, many persons grow up still fooling themselves, getting by only by covering up for themselves at every turn. Now that you are leaving childhood and beginning to enter adulthood, you can choose more mature ways of dealing with your shortcomings.

One ally you have in trying to own up to your own limitations and faults is your knowledge that no matter how well you fool yourself (and even your friends), you are not able to fool God, who knows you even better than you know yourself. A psalmist once cried out when he realized how very well God knew him:

**O God, thou knowest my folly;
the wrongs I have done are not hidden from thee.
(Ps. 69:5.)**

We know that God's love continues even when he knows our foolishness. Even though we try to trick ourselves into thinking we are better than we are, or more certain than we are, God knows how foolish we are, and he still loves us. If even our folly cannot make him stop loving us, then why do we think we need to fool anyone, even ourselves? If God loves us and accepts us as his children, why must we pretend anymore, wearing masks to make ourselves and those around us think we are important, or smart, or sure of everything?

The answer is simple. *We don't have to.* And realizing that we need to be only ourselves—without the funny masks of pretend-I'm-someone-else—is a big part of accepting God's love for us. He loves and accepts us as he made us; we can learn to accept ourselves too!

O God, help me be myself. When I try to trick myself and those I love, pretending to be what I am not, forgive me, and love me back into my own selfhood again. In Jesus' name. AMEN.

85

you can learn to be . . .

An All-Weather Friend

DO YOU HAVE AN ALL-WEATHER COAT? WHETHER YOU do or not, you know that an all-weather coat is just that—a coat you can wear in all kinds of weather the year 'round.

If it's raining, snowing, or sleeting, the fabric of your coat repels the moisture. If the weather's warm, you can unzip the lining—presto!—you have a light-weight coat. Some all-weather coats are reversible, too. You can turn the coat inside out, and the lining be-comes a bright woolly coat for frosty mornings or eve-nings.

The all-weather coat is much like the true friend. No matter what happens, a true friend is always there, ready to share your sorrows, your joys, your ex-periences—good or bad. On the other hand, the fair-weather friend disappears when the going gets tough, when difficulties come along. He is interested only in what you have—popularity, use of the car, a good allow-ance, interesting friends, and so forth. He has little real interest in you as a person—in what you really are, in what he can contribute to your friendship.

Of course anyone can judge his friends. He can say to himself that Joe is a fair-weather friend, Betty is an all-weather friend, Bill is—well, maybe we're not sure. But when we begin thinking about our friends, we have to think about ourselves too. It takes at least two people to make a friendship. So we have to begin asking such questions as these:

What kind of friend am I? Am I a fair-weather friend? Or can my friends depend on me—know that I am an all-weather friend? What can I do to let them know that I am trying to be a true friend?

There is a classic story of an all-weather friendship in the Bible. Perhaps you would like to read and think about it today. You will find it in I Samuel 18:1-4; 20:35-42.

There are friends who pretend to be friends,
but there is a friend who sticks closer than a brother.
(Prov. 18:24.)

Help me grow, Father, in my friendships. I want to be the kind of person friends can depend on—an all-weather friend. Strengthen me to stand by them when difficulties arise for my friends and when I want to turn my back and run. Keep me from pretending to them, from using them for my own selfish ends. I pray in Jesus' name. AMEN.

when you're full of . . .

Excuses, Excuses, Excuses!

IF THE FIRST VERY PRIMITIVE LIGHT BULB HAD BEEN withheld from the public because it wasn't perfect, many people would have lived their lives in the dark. Only when the funny little glass tube could be tried out could Mr. Edison find out what was wrong with it and thus begin to correct it. Since the light bulb wasn't perfect, Mr. Edison had a good excuse not to let the world have such a fragile, imperfect tool. But he didn't withhold it. The men and women who benefitted from its light and warmth must be grateful that he didn't.

Offering the talent and contribution you have now enables you to grow further and contribute even more as a result. But it is tempting, especially in your youth, to decide you don't have much to offer, or that you aren't ready "yet" to make a contribution. Moses faced that temptation when God first asked him to do a job.

Read the story in the third and fourth chapters of Exodus.

He was a shepherd in the desert at the time and he met God one day when he saw a bush afire that was not being burned up. From the bush came God's voice. It was a voice Moses did not want to hear, for it commanded him to return to Egypt and force Pharaoh to let the Hebrew people leave their land of bondage and seek a free home.

Moses started giving excuses—the very excuses you have used at times. Excuses like these:

"But why are you asking me to do it?" (God's answer: Because I have asked you to, and I will be helping you.)

"But nobody wants to listen to me—they know I don't have anything to say." (God's answer: I will give you help in persuading them that I have sent you. You will be representing me.)

"But you know I'm not very clever at things like that —I can't make a speech to a king." (God's answer: Well then, I'll send someone along to help you. And I'll be helping both of you do your jobs.)

Most of the excuses we make have answers like those God gave Moses. When we are being called to serve God's purposes, we need to think carefully before we pull back with feeble protests as Moses did. We ought to be encouraged by the fact that God recognized Moses' limitations. Since Moses couldn't be very eloquent (do you suppose he stuttered, or was just afraid when he was in front of important people?), God found

Aaron, his brother, and commanded him to go along to make the speeches that Moses would plan.

You can be sure your own weaknesses will be matched by the strengths of others, and your talents, limited as you might think they are, will play an important role in God's kingdom.

But first you must be willing. No excuses!

Help me, God, to do my part—at home—at school— in the neighborhood. Help me learn to offer my talents to you, and remind me that you can use even my weakest abilities to perform your work on earth. In Jesus' name I pray. AMEN.

learning to place . . .

Christ Above All

"WANTED—YOUNG, SKINNY, WIRY FELLOWS NOT OVER 18. Must be expert riders, willing to risk death daily. Orphans preferred. Wages, $25 a week."

This strange ad appeared in a San Francisco paper, and the men who answered it became the first of the famed Pony Express riders. Young, skinny, wiry fellows *were* needed, and they'd best be expert riders willing to risk death daily, for the trail from St. Joseph, Missouri, to Sacramento, California, was untamed and demanding. But why were "orphans preferred"? Because they had only themselves to think about. They could give their full attention and their whole loyalty to their job. As we know, the eighty orphans who answered the ad did just that. Challenged by one of the toughest jobs in the world, they gave themselves wholeheartedly to carrying the mail. The plains, the desert, and the mountains, with their threat of death by blazing sun or avalanching snow, were conquered.

Every age has its own hard-as-rock problems to be tackled, and throughout history we have been finding ways to solve them. The persons most likely to do their part find out how to face every moment with the abandon and surrender of the Pony Express rider, giving their whole loyalty to the work they are doing, refusing to be held back by loyalties that limit their outlook. Once when Jesus was trying to straighten out the disciples' ideas about himself, he said to them:

Do not think that I have come to bring peace on earth; I have not come to bring peace, but a sword. For I have come to set a man against his father, and a daughter against her mother, and a daughter-in-law against her mother-in-law; and a man's foes will be those of his own household. He who loves father or mother more than me is not worthy of me; and he who loves son or daughter more than me is not worthy of me; and he who does not take up his cross and follow

91

me is not worthy of me. He who finds his life will lose
it, and he who loses his life for my sake will find it.
(Matt. 10:34-39.)

Another time Jesus said to the men who had given
up everything to follow him:

Truly, I say to you, there is no man who has left
house or wife or brothers or parents or children, for the
sake of the kingdom of God, who will not receive mani-
fold more in this time, and in the age to come eternal
life. (Luke 18:29-30.)

Jesus was not really saying that family loyalty is
bad, but he was exaggerating in order to say to his
disciples: When you answer my call, remember that you
may be asked to give up everything that means much
to you. The things you value most, even your family,
must take second place to my command. If you are
going to do my work, you must be ready to be loyal
to me alone, ready to risk death daily.

Even though he did not use the language of the Pony
Express ad, he was getting at the same point; orphans
are preferred—those persons who have learned to be
themselves, loyal first to God, carrying his message
to the world.

*O God, help me become a mature Christian, standing
on my own feet, loyal always to Christ, in whose name
I pray.* AMEN.

making friends may depend on . . .

Just a Little Thing

A HUGE MOVING VAN WAS STUCK IN THE ENTRANCE OF an underpass one day. The driver's estimate of the height of the opening was off just a few inches, and the truck could neither go forward nor back out. Within minutes police had arrived, and a large crowd had gathered. Engineers were called to advise on the best way to free the truck. In the midst of all the noise and excitement a small boy made his way to the truck driver.

"I can tell you how to get it out, Mister," he said.

"Okay, Okay. So can everybody else," said the driver impatiently.

"Just let the air out of the tires."

And that's exactly what they did. Those few inches made the difference, and the truck moved smoothly through the underpass. The solution of the problem was such a little thing—so simple that it had been overlooked.

Sometimes the solutions to our problems are like that —just one little thing, one little change, might do the trick. Take this matter of friendship, for example. We all want our classmates to like us, to be popular with our friends. But often some little thing holds us back. We are stuck where we are, and we can't go forward making friends. And very often the reason we are stuck is just a little thing. If we would make just one small change in ourselves, we would become more interesting, more likable persons, and it would be easier to make good friends.

Could it just be that we are a little conceited, that we think more of ourselves than we should? Certainly this won't make friends for us. Nobody likes a stuck-up.

Could it be that we have some habits that turn friends away from us—a habit of criticizing others, or making catty remarks behind their backs, or saying things to make them feel foolish in front of others? Nobody likes to be laughed at.

Or could it be that we do not have a genuine interest in others—that we are really only interested in ourselves? Do we honestly like to see our friends win honors and recognition? Are we honestly happy when good luck comes their way? And do we let them know we are interested in them and happy for them?

We have to take time out every once in a while and try to look at ourselves as our friends look at us. We have to face ourselves honestly and check to see if there is anything in us that is holding us back, keeping us from making the friendships we want and need. Then we have to ask for God's help and truly make those changes in ourselves.

Spend some time in honest self-examination today.

Is there anything about me I can change—my attitudes, my habits, my manner, my appearance—so that I can make friends more easily and can be a good friend? Where do I start in making this change?

Never act from motives of rivalry or personal vanity, but in humility think more of one another than you do of yourselves. None of you should think only of his own affairs, but each should learn to see things from other people's point of view. (Phil. 2:3-4, Phillips.)

O God, help me to be honest with myself—to recognize in myself whatever it is that is holding me back in making and keeping friends. Show me how to overcome my weaknesses and change myself into a more lovable person. AMEN.

when you ask yourself . . .

How Do I Love Me?

NARCISSUS WAS A HANDSOME YOUTH ACCORDING TO
the legends of Greece—and his good looks got him into
trouble. One day as he knelt to drink water from a
pool, he saw himself in the smooth mirror of the surface
—and fell in love with his own beauty! He was so
stricken with himself that he would not eat, drink, or
sleep, and he pined away until at last he died, staring at
the shimmering image of himself.

The sad thing about Narcissus is that he was not
even in love with *himself*—just with a mere *image* of
himself! Every mature person, young or old, if he is
seeking to live as a Christian, knows that he must learn
to love himself. But he also knows that the wrong kind
of self-love can destroy him.

Do you remember the story about the lawyer who
asked Jesus to tell him which law was the greatest?

**You shall love the Lord your God with all your heart,
and with all your soul, and with all your mind. This is
the great and first commandment. And a second is like
it, You shall love your neighbor as yourself. (Matt.
22:37-39.)**

96

It is clear that Jesus was saying that we must learn to love God and our neighbor—*just as we have to learn to love ourselves.*

And how do we learn to love ourselves? A famous psychologist, Carl Rogers, says that most of us have a great deal of trouble accepting or loving ourselves. In fact, he says, of all the thousands of persons he has talked to about their problems, "the great majority despise themselves, regard themselves as worthless and unlovable."

That must sound familiar!

All of us growl at ourselves at times—when we know we've been the cause of lots of family fussing or when we have got someone else in trouble by refusing to take the blame that rightly was ours. But our faith in God's love, as it has been shown us by Jesus' teachings and in the life he lived, keeps us from hating ourselves. We know that God sent his Son to remind us that God loves us. *And if he loves us, then we are not free to despise ourselves. If God loves us even when we are unlovable—and he does—then we can be reassured that our lives are worthwhile, that our feelings of worthlessness do not tell the whole story.* And because we are so grateful to God for loving and providing for us, we return that love to him by finding ways to serve the people around us, his children—by finding ways to express his love in what we say and do.

97

O God, thank you for your love that is never taken away, no matter how worthless I feel. Help me learn to love myself so that I can become the kind of person you want me to be, serving all those around me, so I can thank you for loving me first. In Jesus' name I pray. AMEN.

Prayers

For This Day

My God, I offer to Thee this day
All that I can think, or do, or say;
Uniting it with what was done
On earth by Jesus Christ, Thy son.

AMEN.[3]

For the New Day

My Lord, I am ready on the threshold of this new
day to go forth armed with Thy power, seeking adventure on the high road, to right wrong, to overcome evil,
to serve Thee bravely, faithfully, joyously. AMEN.[4]

For Another Day

As a bird in meadows fair
Or in lonely forest sings,
Till it fills the summer air
And the greenwood sweetly rings,
So my heart to thee would raise,
O my God, its song of praise,
That the gloom of night is o'er
And I see the sun once more.

Bless today whate'er I do,
Bless whate'er I have and love;
From the paths of virtue true
Let me never, never rove;
By thy Spirit strengthen me
In the faith that leads to thee,
Then an heir of life on high
Fearless I may live and die. AMEN.[5]

Before I Sleep

Thanks for today, God . . . for all of it:
  For the friends I saw . . .
  For the beauty around me . . .
  For work to do. . . .
Thanks for today, God . . . for all of it:
  For mistakes discovered . . .
  For sins forgiven . . .
  For angry words unspoken. . . .
Thanks for today, God . . . for all of it, every bit.
                                        AMEN.

For Forgiveness

O God, so often we start out in the morning meaning
to be good. We want to be clean and joyous and helpful

102

all day. Then something happens, and first thing we know, we've spoken an unkind word and made a shadow come across somebody's face. Or we've done something we're ashamed of. What makes us like that, God? We're sorry and ashamed.

Somehow we feel You understand; You know what's weak inside us—make us strong. Forgive us, and help us to be understanding and forgiving toward others that may hurt us. Help us learn to love, from the bigness of Your love. AMEN.[6]

Before I Leave for School

Today, O Lord, remind me
   to be myself with everyone I meet;
   to offer myself to serve those who need me;
   to concentrate on the work I have to do;
   to return home wiser and truer. AMEN.

Teach Me to Play

Teach me, O Lord, to play!

Others have taught me the rules. But do thou teach me the inner spirit.

Let me learn of thee to throw all that I have into the game I play. For this has always been thy will.

Grant me skill to play well. For mind and nerve and muscle from which skill comes are thy gifts to me.

Enable me, my Lord, to play fairly, and always with honor. For whence come the laws of all fair dealing but from thee?

Make me chivalrous to my opponents, loyal to my companions, and generous in giving praise. For these are the qualities that thou hast blessed in the dealings of men with each other everywhere.

Thus I come to thee, my Lord, to learn the spirit of play. For I know that thou hast made play a part of this world of thine. AMEN.[7]

For Control

Help me, O God, to control my tongue. Keep me from telling lies, from gossiping, from making harsh remarks that cut and sting. Help me to hold back the words of anger and name-calling. Instead, teach me to speak truthfully, gently, and in Christian love, whatever my feelings inside may be. AMEN.

For Strength

Our Father, may the world not mold us today, but may we be so strong as to help to mold the world.
AMEN.[8]

For Deep Waters

We thank thee, our Father, for peaceful rivers
   on whose surface ripples dance in the sunlight,
   whose calm bays reflect the beauty of over-
     hanging branches,
   whose stillness is a balm for tired hearts.
We thank thee for singing rivers
   that babble over stones in the brookbed,
   that dash over rocks on the hillside
   and splash down steep waterfalls.
   These bring gaiety to our dull routine.
We thank thee, Lord, for mighty rivers
   that turn the great wheels of industry,
   on which the riverboats glide toward the sea
   and open new worlds to us.
We thank thee, O God, for living waters
   along whose banks the cattle graze,
   the trees give shelter to the birds,
   crops ripen in the fertile soil,
     and we are blessed. AMEN.[9]

For Good Leaders

O God, send us leaders who aren't too easy on us—
who hold up before us things to do that are entirely too
hard for us (but we *try,* anyway!), . . . who let us

know in no uncertain terms that they expect nothing less than our best (and they always seem to expect more than *we* think is our best), . . . who show us what it is to be strong, and not to give in to little disappointments or pains and aches or failures (and by their own strength, we seem to have more ourselves). Send us, O God, leaders who are *good* for us! AMEN.[10]

To Be a Christian

Our God and King, we pray thee this day for courage:
Courage to be unpopular for the sake of truth and sincerity;
Courage to risk our lives in a cause that is greater than life;
Courage to declare our convictions at whatever cost to ourselves;
Courage to trust the truth, even when the battle seems to go against it;
Courage to be alone with thee in the right;
Courage to admit when we are wrong;
Courage to start anew when we have fallen;
Courage to do our best and leave the outcome in the hands of God;
Courage to walk with Christ along a lonely road;
Courage to be a Christian. AMEN.[11]

If Your Friends Say You're Touchy

Lord, my feelings
are always getting hurt. Some of my friends say
I'm touchy, too easily offended;
my parents tell me I'm oversensitive. Often
   I'm sure
I'm being laughed at,
or gossiped about,
or unfairly criticized.
I imagine "digs" in even casual comments
about my clothes, my appearance, or my common
   sense.
I need thy help, Father, in conquering
this weakness. Jar me out of my
self-absorption. Save me from thinking about
myself so much, and help me to mingle with my
   friends
in warm-hearted ways. AMEN.[12]

When a New Year Begins

I wonder, God, what I will make of the year ahead?
You know the problems and troubles and limitations
I carry with me into this new year. Can you lead me in
ways that will enable me to live closer to your guidance,
to walk straighter in your way, and to rest surer in your

love? Can you take even my life and use it? I offer myself to you—such a small gift. Can you use me? In Jesus' name I pray. AMEN.

When Summer Comes

In the leisurely days ahead, Dear God, help me find signs of thee all along the way. In the friendships I form, and in the games I play, as well as in the work I do, let me see thy handiwork and be moved to praise thee for thy loving-kindness. In the name of Christ.

AMEN.

At Christmas Time

Our Father, we rejoice and give thanks for thy great love declared in the birth of Jesus on that night in Bethlehem so long ago. As we celebrate his birth again this year, bring us to a deeper understanding of what love really means. Following his example, we would express love, deep and sincere, in all our relationships —not just at Christmas time, but every day. We pray in Jesus' name. AMEN.[13]

Before Communion

O God, my Father, as I prepare to come to thy table, I stop to thank thee for thy love of me. I know that love is with me always—even when I have deserted thee and gone my own way. Help me today to renew my faith in thee. May the body and blood of Christ give me new courage to walk in his ways. AMEN.

A Prayer of Dedication

Fill us, we pray Thee, with thy light and life, that we may show forth thy wondrous glory. Grant that thy love may so fill our lives that we may count nothing too small to do for Thee, nothing too much to give, and nothing too hard to bear. So teach us, Lord, to serve thee as thou deservest, to give and not to count the cost, to fight and not to heed the wounds, to toil and not to seek for rest, to labor and not to ask for any reward save that of knowing that we do thy will. AMEN.[14]

Sources

1. By Amado Nervo in *The World at One in Prayer,* edited by Daniel J. Fleming (New York: Harper & Brothers, 1942), pp. 17-18.
2. From "Swinging on a Star," by Johnny Burke and Jimmy Heusen.
3. By Clifton B. Cates in *The Armed Forces Prayer Book,* edited by Daniel A. Poling (New York: Prentice-Hall, Inc., 1951), p. 19.
4. On a knight's tomb, Church Icomb, England (thirteenth century).
5. A German hymn translated by Catherine Winkworth (1829-78).
6. Clarice M. Bowman, *Worship Ways for Camp* (New York: Association Press, 1955), p. 150.
7. Percy R. Hayward, *Young People's Prayers* (A Keen-Age Reflection Book; New York: Association Press, 1945), p. 27.
8. J. H. Jowett (nineteenth century).
9. Dorothy Wells Pease, *Inspiration Under the Sky* (Nashville: Abingdon Press, 1963), p. 25.
10. Clarice M. Bowman, *Worship Ways for Camp,* p. 148.
11. By Owen M. Geer in *Workshop,* November, 1946.
12. Walter L. Cook, *Daily Life Prayers for Youth* (New York: Association Press, 1963), p. 45.
13. Helen F. Couch and Sam S. Barefield, *Worship Sourcebook for Youth* (Nashville: Abingdon Press, 1962), p. 255.
14. A prayer of Loyola.
